T0402804

THE SCIENCE OF FAIRY TALES

A JUST-RIGHT BED

AND THE SCIENCE OF

GOLDILOCKS AND THE THREE BEARS

WRITTEN BY MONICA CLARK-ROBINSON
ILLUSTRATED BY DUSAN PAVLIC

PICTURE WINDOW BOOKS
a capstone imprint

The Scientific Method

1. Ask a Question

Ask yourself, "What do I want to learn more about?" or "I wonder what would happen if . . . ?"

2. Form a Hypothesis

Make a prediction or an educated guess about what might happen.

3. Experiment

Test your hypothesis by making a plan and conducting an experiment.

4. Observe and Record

Make careful observations during your experiment and write down what you see.

5. Analyze the Data

Collect and study the results of your data. Was your hypothesis correct?

6. Draw a Conclusion

Make your conclusion and share your results.

First things first: I was neither lost nor hungry. And please don't call me Goldilocks. I'm Golda Locke, and I work to make Storyland better using science. My new project is researching the animals of Storyland to learn about their behaviors.

On the day I was planning to research the Three Bears, I forgot my scientific equipment. I would just have to use the power of observation and the scientific method for my research.

The bears weren't home, but the gate was unlocked . . .

. . . so I let myself in and looked around for a spot to wait. There were three chairs in the living room. I would use the science of observation to determine which chair to sit on.

The first one looked way too big and way too hard.

The second one looked a little too big and a little too soft.

The third one looked just right. Based on my observations, I decided to try the third chair.

After all, you can't go wrong with science . . .

I headed to the kitchen and found three bowls of porridge. Bowl one was steaming hot—much too hot!

Bowl two was topped with frozen berries and cold—much too cold.

Bowl three wasn't steaming hot and didn't have frozen berries. It looked just right. I had a little taste, for science . . .

After that yummy porridge, I needed a rest. I went upstairs and found three beds. Unlike the chairs, I tested all of these. The big bed was too hard.

The medium bed was too soft.

The smallest bed was just right, so I settled in for a nap.
But as soon as I laid down, I couldn't stop thinking.

No way could I rest until I had the answer. With my trusty notebook in hand and the scientific method on my side, I got to work!

QUESTION
Why do the beds feel different?

HYPOTHESIS
Each bed is made from different materials that vary in softness.

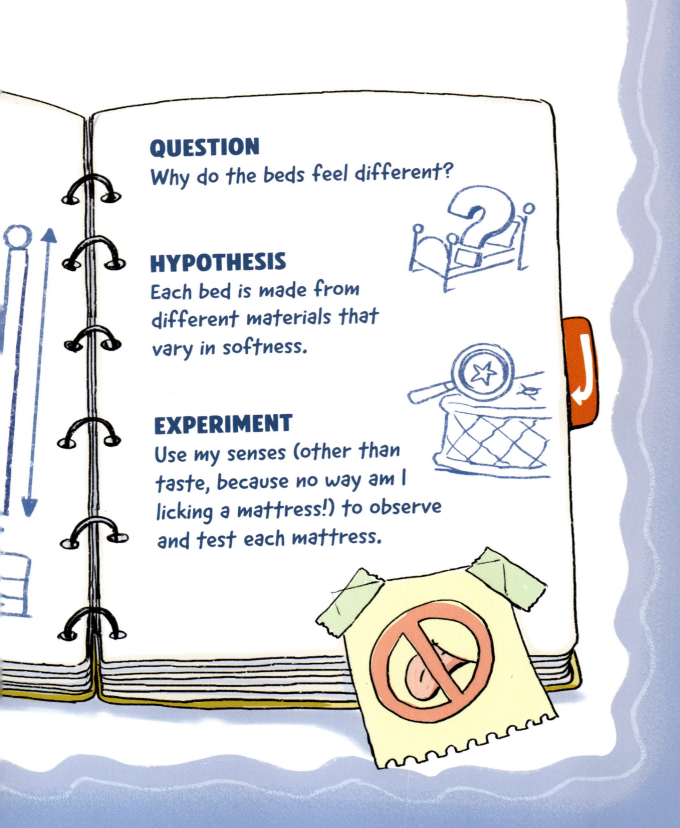

EXPERIMENT
Use my senses (other than taste, because no way am I licking a mattress!) to observe and test each mattress.

BIG mattress

Looks: overstuffed
Feels: hard but springy
Smells: like nothing
Sounds: squeaky

Squeak!

MEDIUM mattress
Looks: fluffy
Feels: soft and a little
pokey
Smells: like bird feathers
Sounds: like nothing

SMALL mattress

Looks: comfy
Feels: firm but soft
Smells: like fresh hay
Sounds: crunchy

Then I **ANALYZED** the data, or information, and made an educated guess on the materials in each bed.

With my question answered, I finally fell asleep. I had barely started snoozing when I heard voices.

"Look, Papa," a small voice said. "Someone broke my chair."

Soon, I heard footsteps on the stairs.

After the bears stopped screaming, I introduced myself.
"I'm Golda Locke. I'm researching all the animals in Storyland,
and you're next on my list. I left you a message about it."

"Oh yes," Mama Bear said. "We'd love to hear more about
your project."

We chatted about my research all afternoon.

"How did you know which bowl of porridge was just right to eat?" Baby Bear asked.

"Let's make some porridge and use the scientific method to find out," I replied.

QUESTION
Can you tell if the porridge is too hot or too cold to eat without trying it?

HYPOTHESIS
Yes! You can tell by using your senses and observations.

EXPERIMENT: Make three bowls of porridge and add different toppings to each one.

Pour hot milk into the first bowl.

Add frozen berries to the second bowl.

Add nuts to the third bowl.

"We'll use our senses to **OBSERVE** each bowl. We'll **RECORD** our discoveries as we go," I explained.

We felt the sides of each bowl. We looked for steam coming from the porridge. We examined the extra ingredients.

"Now we need to **ANALYZE** our data, taste each bowl, and draw our **CONCLUSION**," I said.

"This one is just right!" Baby Bear exclaimed. "Our hypothesis was correct!"

"Science is all about answering questions,"
I told Baby Bear.

So, what about YOU, scientists?
What are YOUR questions?

I used the power of observation before sitting on the smallest chair, but my observation was off.

Let's try a new experiment. This time, let's use a box as a chair. Instead of observation, let's test the weight of some objects.

QUESTION: Can I use a big box as a chair?

HYPOTHESIS: If the box holds 20 big books it will hold me.

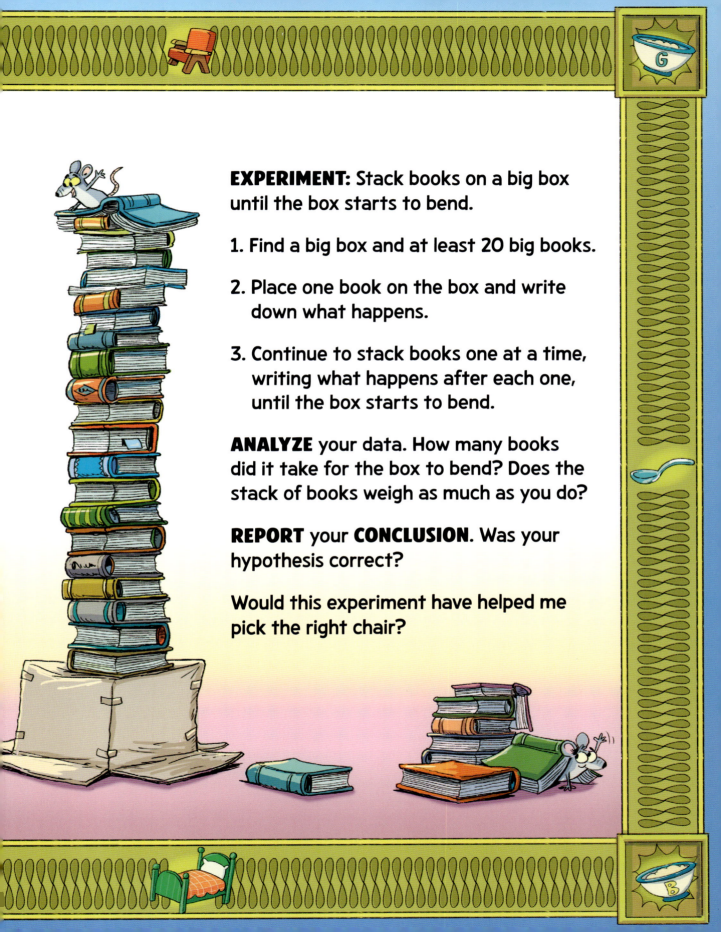

EXPERIMENT: Stack books on a big box until the box starts to bend.

1. Find a big box and at least 20 big books.

2. Place one book on the box and write down what happens.

3. Continue to stack books one at a time, writing what happens after each one, until the box starts to bend.

ANALYZE your data. How many books did it take for the box to bend? Does the stack of books weigh as much as you do?

REPORT your **CONCLUSION**. Was your hypothesis correct?

Would this experiment have helped me pick the right chair?

MEET THE AUTHOR

Monica Clark-Robinson is passionately in love with the stories that connect us across culture, race, and age. She believes the right story, at the right time, can change a person's life. When not writing, Monica is a professional actor and voice-over artist and loves to cook and garden. She lives in a yurt in the country with one spouse, too many cats, and just the right amount of daughters.

Photo: Miroslav Milić

MEET THE ILLUSTRATOR

Dusan Pavlic has illustrated hundreds of books for publishers around the world. Many of his witty and charming illustrations have won awards, including the Golden Pen. Dusan works as an illustrator and graphic designer in Belgrade, Serbia.

Published by Picture Window Books, an imprint of Capstone
1710 Roe Crest Drive, North Mankato, Minnesota 56003
capstonepub.com

Library of Congress Cataloging-in-Publication Data is available on the Library of Congress website.
ISBN: 9798875216541 (hardcover)
ISBN: 9798875216497 (paperback)
ISBN: 9798875216503 (ebook PDF)

Summary: Golda Locke (also known as Goldilocks) explains what really happened when she visited the home of the Three Bears, and science plays a major role in this retelling.

Editor: Christianne Jones
Designer: Sarah Bennett
Production Specialist: Katy LaVigne

Printed and bound in China. 6274